Lynn Dutrow

OOK

ALIGNED
as f★ck

Your companion for taking the action steps necessary to transform your inner assholes* into allies

*LIKE ANXIETY

EXPLANATIONS, EXAMPLES, AND KICKASS ACTION STEPS

Copyright © 2023 Lynn Dutrow

All Rights Reserved

Year of the Book
135 Glen Avenue
Glen Rock, PA 17327

ISBN: 978-1-64649-362-3

*While I am a Licensed Clinical Professional Counselor, this
content is not intended to provide mental health treatment and is
not a replacement for the therapeutic relationship in psychotherapy
or the coaching relationship. Always seek the advice of your own
Medical Provider and/or Mental Health Provider regarding questions
or concerns you have about your specific health or medications,
herbs, or supplements. If you have or suspect that you have a
medical or mental health problem, contact your own Medical
Provider or Mental Health Provider promptly.*

Printed in the United States of America.

Cover and book design by Solveig Petch at petchy.co.

To all of the Wise Women
who supported me, guided me, and
shared their wealth of wisdom with
me — I aspire to do the same
through sharing my wisdom, wit,
and words with you

Preamble

*"We, the Inner Assholes,
in order to form a protective entity
to keep you alive"*

Yeah, that may have been funnier in my head.

Here's the deal about this AaF Companion Workbook. The Aligned As F*ck book has 7 chapters with 3 concepts per chapter – plus some bonuses – so there are a total of 24 concepts. You were given an action step in each chapter. I understand that you may, or may not, have put all of the concepts into action.

Your Inner Assholes have been attempting to protect you (because that is essentially their job) and they are not going down without a fight. Taking Action is key to any transformation, so here are even more examples and actions steps for you to use as tools on your journey.

This workbook is the antidote to your bullshit excuses. There is an action step spelled out for every concept.

As part of the writing process I took thirteen people on a guided tour through this workbook. Their feedback asked for "more examples" and "more clear directions." You will find plenty of both inside.

Now for directions as to how to use this workbook...
I've been doing this work for more years than we are going to count, and I have so much knowledge and experience accrued. When it is mixed with my excitement, it's easy to overwhelm a new client or reader. I often joke that if I could find a way to open up a client's cranium and pour in all of that wisdom and experience at one time, I would. Since no one has figured out how to do that (yet), it's important for us to pace ourselves. The same goes for the information shared here.

Digest it at a pace that works for you.

While I kept to the letters of the word A.L.I.G.N.E.D. in writing both the book and workbook, there is no requirement that you read the chapters in strict order. I would suggest that you start with the first chapter "A". Some activities do build upon previous ones. In some you will find strong encouragement to "lather, rinse, and repeat" them. Skip around if that works best for you.

If you haven't figured it out yet, your Inner Assholes might attempt to sabotage your reading of this book by telling you that there is a "right" way to approach the reading and action steps inside. While I would recommend reading in order, you have my permission, if you need it, to do it whatever way works best for you!

While it is not entirely necessary for you to have read the original book in order to gain insight and take action by using this workbook, I do strongly encourage you to use the book and workbook together. There is really good shit in both of them and they are easier to understand and digest if you pair them.

Think of them as wine and cheese or peanut butter and chocolate. Each can stand on their own AND they are clearly better together.

One last note before we jump in together. Doing this work is not easy. What I shared in the original book and in this workbook are suggestions. They are intended to encourage you to think in ways you may not have in your past, to bring you a new perspective, and to support you in making the work easier. While I am a Licensed Mental Health provider, this material is not intended to take the place of the support and guidance of a professional.

This material may bring up some deep shit for you. Do not attempt to tough it out or go on alone. Seek support.

— Lynn D.

I created this workbook to be your companion for taking the action steps necessary to transform your inner assholes (like anxiety) into allies.

What you'll find inside:

- Acknowledge
- Accept
- Anthropomorphize
- Bonus "A" Awareness
- Extra Special Bonus Action Step
- Watch Your Language
- Lean In
- Lead
- Bonus "L" Love Letters
- Illuminate
- Inspire
- Core Values List
- Ignite
- Get Over It
- Get On With It
- Go Take Action
- No Means No, Not Maybe
- No Judgment
- No Excuses
- Embrace the Process
- Embarrassment Won't Kill You
- Enter Humor Stage Left
- Discern
- Decide
- Deal with It or Delegate It or Dump It

Acknowledge

Accept

Anthropomorphize

Bonus "A" Awareness

Extra Special Bonus Action Step

Acknowledge

ac·knowl·edge

/əkˈnäləj/

verb

1. accept or admit the existence or truth of.
    "the plight of the refugees was acknowledged by the authorities"

    Similar: admit, accept, grant, allow, concede, confess, own, appreciate, recognize, realize, respect, cooperate with, cognize

    Opposite: reject, deny

2. (of a body of opinion) recognize the fact or importance or quality of.
    "the art world has begun to acknowledge his genius"

To acknowledge is to take action. It is a verb. By simply admitting, accepting, granting, and allowing... you are already taking an action step. You don't have to like your Inner Assholes (yet... or ever), but you do have to acknowledge that they are a part of you and allow them space.

Denying their existence or unilaterally rejecting their suggestions will keep you stuck on the same endless loop that sucks your time, energy, and any hope of feeling joy right out of you.

If that's how you want to spend the rest of your one shot at this life you have been gifted, then walk away now, because what I am suggesting will just piss you off...

Your Inner Assholes have a job to do: Protect you! They are just overzealous and obnoxious in their interpretation and execution of their perceived job description.

When your Inner Assholes show up, you may be tempted to go the route of bullying them back with statements like "Get the fuck away from me, asshole" or with submissive statements like "Yes Master, of course I believe you and will do whatever you want" while cowering in the corner or overdoing until you are overwhelmed.

*There is another great example of this on page 20 in Aligned As F*ck.*

Part one of this Action Step is to write down what you might say (bullying or submissive) that does NOT seem to work well with your Inner Assholes:

If you are feeling stuck, here are some more examples and you can simply circle one that resonates with you:

Go away, asshole   **Leave me alone**   **Ew, you stink**

Fuck off!   **You're annoying**

Do I really have to?
Yes, do it right now, damnit!

Part two of this Action Step is to notice when your Inner Assholes show up and just say, "Hey there," or some other neutral phrase that does not add gasoline to their fire.

Some examples that were shared during the editing groups include, "Nobody bothers me" (from an old martial arts commercial), "Not Today," or even a non-verbal pat on the head as a loving gesture to your Inner Assholes, like a pet who is interrupting your work AND who you are not going to play with in that moment!

What is a neutral response that you are willing to use as a response when your Inner Assholes show up? (You can circle one of the examples on the previous page if that works better for you.)

What I will say (or do) when my Inner Assholes show up that acknowledges them without giving them power over me:

Accept

"Accept" is sometimes confused with "except" — *Challenge Accepted*

This is a tough one because our brains would rather except (not include) rather than accept (welcome) our Inner Assholes. Rejecting, refusing, and turning them down seems to make logical sense. They are "bad," right? What have we been taught and conditioned to do with "bad" things? Get rid of them, stay away from them, reject them.

So I know it goes against your conditioning and what seems to make sense AND I'm going to ask you to trust me on this one. Your Inner Assholes are not "bad." They are simply misguided. They are the parts of you that are being overprotective, like your own personal Secret Service agents, with sour expressions, who are using their power to intimidate you. It just makes their job easier when you cower and bow to them.

So stand up, brush yourself off, and decide that they are about to get an ass whipping!

Wait, that won't work. Bullying a bully just perpetuates the problem.

Let's take a page out of ACT (Acceptance and Commitment Therapy) and choose to accept your Inner Assholes rather than dwell on their negativity. Stop wrestling in their mud and stay on shore. Observe them without engaging in their game.

The most important aspect of accepting your Inner Assholes is to stop fighting with them. They will work hard to distract you with thoughts of the past or the future. When you know their game and choose not to play it, you will find yourself more often in the present moment, which is the only moment in which you have any power to make a change. **Your Inner Assholes are neither your boss nor your enemy.**

Acceptance may be one of the most challenging concepts in this whole process of transformation AND one of the most powerful ones, too. Rather than reiterating and being redundant here, I do encourage you to refer to page 21 in Aligned As F*ck for more information about the history and importance of accepting the less than shiny parts of yourself.

Since this concept of Acceptance is deep and challenging I will go a little bit easy on you for this Action Step. You simply have to sign that you are committing to acceptance.

Choose to allow your Inner Assholes a place at your table. Be willing to meet them, greet them, allow them out into the light, be willing to get to know them, and keep an open mind.

> ☐ *I am willing to acknowledge my Inner Assholes and do the work to transform them into Allies.* SIGNATURE _____

Anthropomorphize

Now the simultaneously fun and frustrating next step... It's time to put a face to those fuckers!

Here is where we are going to dig into one of the most critical action steps in this process of transforming your Inner Assholes: Naming them. Not just naming them. Putting a face and a backstory to them as well.

Allow me to sidebar for a moment... As you approach this Action Step, keep in mind that your Inner Assholes have a job to do—protect you. They are like your own personal Secret Service agents. Trouble is, there is confusion about who is the boss, you or them. They are overzealous and will use whatever tactics they deem necessary to keep you safe. Most of the time they are overreacting. Working through these action steps is a process for clearing up the confusion of who is in charge. (In case you were curious, YOU are in charge.)

It's time to get to know your Inner Assholes at least as well as you know your best friend. If you haven't made a new friend since Kindergarten, let me walk you through the process.

Start by being open to making a new friend, or two, or ten! Then take notice of possible candidates for your open friendship slot. You have already acknowledged and accepted that you have a head partially filled with Inner Assholes. Let's just go ahead and call them "candidates." Here's where you dig in to this Action Step. Ask for their name.

Your Inner Assholes have been hanging out for years, so there is no need for any more parallel play. It's time to name them and then sort out their backstory. If they are playing hard to get, you can give them a nickname. **Some of mine are:**

Inner Critic	⇥	**Great Aunt Busybody**
Anxiety	⇥	**Mucinex Monster** (Muci for short)
Voice of Doubt	⇥	**VoD**
Impostor	⇥	**Milli Vanilli**
Perfectionist	⇥	**Persephone**

Examples of what clients have called their Inner Assholes:

Dementors	*Peggy*
Bogarts	*Simon Says*
Slimer	*Bruno*
Angie	*Bitter Betty*
Hedgehog	*Tsu (short for Tsunami)*
Karen	*Tynnyfer (nickname for the Tasmanian Devil)*
Richard (Dick)	*Fuck Face*
Prissy Pants	*Ursula (with her invasive tentacles)*
Regina George (Mean Girls)	*Felix Felicis*
Candy (the Cruise Director)	
Olga (the overworker)	

This naming step seems to be the one that most people attempt to skip over. You have free will so are welcome to skip this Action Step. However, I will not guarantee that any of the other steps will be as effective if this one is not taken!

Do you have people in your life that you interact with regularly without knowing their names (or at least have a made-up nickname for them)?

The only way to get ALIGNED As F*ck is to be willing to get to know your Inner Assholes by name and learn something about them. That's how it goes in real life. We connect with others by getting to know things about them; we do our best to understand their history, hopes, and aspirations.

Take the time to do this for yourself.

In case it has not been obvious up to this point, your Inner Assholes are aspects of yourself, and this Action Step is asking you to get to know yourself better.

Take your time with this step. It doesn't have to be perfect. You can change their names later, and unlike the real world, you don't have to go through the legal system to do it!

Suggestions for Success with this Step:
Please only work with one Inner Asshole at a time — too many at once will overwhelm you. This is a "lather, rinse, repeat" Action Step. You will come back to it several times, over as long of a period of time as necessary.

Your Inner Assholes can be represented by a character (Chicken Little), a person you know (teacher, coach, great aunt, who was particularly critical), or a random or rhyming name (Angie Anxiety).

There is no right answer here.

Your Inner Perfectionist (mine is Persephone and thinks she is hot shit) may attempt to convince you that this is too hard (and does not like for you to do things you are not good at) and not worth your time. Tell those IAs to take a seat while you dive into the tough stuff!

Do your best to get started and let this work evolve over time.

My Inner Asshole's name is:
(remember to only work with one at a time)

Now that you have a name to work with, it's time to have a visual to go with the name.

Grab your favorite creative medium and draw, doodle, or in whatever way floats your boat, sketch your newly named Inner Asshole.

If this step is really tripping you up, here are some generic characters and you can simply name them. Just get their name and a visual for now. We will get into their backstory in another section.

Bonus A ⟫→ Awareness

Just like when I wrote Aligned As F*ck, something keeps reminding me to talk about the importance of awareness when transforming your life. So consider this a Bonus "A" that includes an Action Step.

Fear is a reaction that you feel in your body, to an actual (at this moment) perceived threat.

Anxiety is a reaction that you feel in your body to a potential, future, possible threat.

Understand the difference?

Fear is part of your survival system and helps your body decide to fight, flee, freeze, or fawn (people-pleasing to avoid conflict) depending on the current situation and what is most likely to keep you alive at that moment.

Anxiety is about anticipating that there might be something that will threaten your survival (or not) in the future.

Awareness is spending more time in the present moment than in the future... or in the past for that matter.

Your Action Step here is to spend more time in the present moment.

It sounds so easy and yet can be so elusive! Here is one way to work on what most would call "mindfulness."

Set an intention to notice when your mind is wandering into the future. Once you are aware of where your mind has wandered, use a vaudeville hook to move that thought or worry about the future to the side and bring your attention back to what is actually going on right where you are in that moment.

Forcing yourself to sit in meditation and think about nothing is probably not working so well for you. Start with this:

"Mindfulness isn't about thinking about nothing, it's about being in charge of what you are thinking about"

Know that you have the power to change your thoughts at any given moment. Your thoughts are not the boss of you!

So practice changing your thoughts, your narrative, your story... Awareness and Action are like the Wonder Twins (I'm a child of the '70s and '80s, so look it up). Put them together and activate your Power!

By signing below you are committing to this Action Step of incorporating more mindfulness and awareness into your day!

> ☐ *I commit to practicing awareness of the present moment as often as I am able to each day.*
>
> SIGNATURE
> _____

Extra special bonus action step

One of the greatest challenges to helping people transform their current situation from "oh fuck" to "fuck yeah" is getting the momentum going to actually take the action steps, rather than just sitting and spinning on them.

Just like I shared earlier, you have free will and are welcome to give in to the part of you that likes the dopamine hit* you got from buying this book, but does not want you to actually take the action steps suggested.

Stay stuck or take action.
The choice is yours.

> * Dopamine is one of our "feel good" neurotransmitters and can be obtained in healthy ways like eating certain healthy foods, exercising, and getting sleep. Less healthy ways are through social media likes, buying the next best thing, and bingeing things like drugs, Netflix, and coffee.

If you want to actually transform your relationship with your Inner Assholes OR you are just a natural overachiever (in which case the previous two paragraphs may not apply to you unless you don't do the action steps because you're too busy overdoing for others) then you will want to put your ass in gear and not only do the regular Action Steps, you will also be eager to do the extra special Bonus Action Step!

Acknowledge, accept, anthropomorphize, awareness

Put all of the "A"s together and write a speech to your Inner Assholes as they make the transition to being your Allies.

Picture a retirement party or, if you want the humor element, one of those "Celebrity Roasts" where the guest of honor is subjected to jokes at their expense.

Thank your Inner Assholes for their service up to this point and share how you are looking forward to your new and improved relationship. Share something specific to each IA that you have identified so far in your process.

While my example lists several of my Inner Assholes, I encourage you to write yours as you identify each Inner Asshole, so that may mean just one or two at a time. Here is an example to inspire you:

Dearest Inner Assholes,

We are gathered here today to mark the beginning of a new era in our relationship. While my promotion to CCA (Chief Compassionate Asskicker) may be a bit unnerving for you, it does also come with some perks for all of us.

Thank you for your years of service protecting me. I recognize that you were doing your best, even if your best often included you using your knowledge, skills, and abilities to torment and torture me in your zealous pursuit to keep me safe from all manner of both actual threats and, more often, perceived threats.

Like the time Great Aunt Busybody berated me for what went wrong with the presentation and told me never to do another presentation, rather than reminding me that it was my first time and that I would have plenty of opportunities to practice and get more proficient over time.

Then there was the time that Muci Monster scared the shit out of me with thoughts about having cancer. That was super fun. Thankfully I fought back and looked at Muci's supposed "evidence" and realized that Muci was not only full of snot, Muci was also full of shit. Even if I did have cancer, I would deal with it. Worrying is not problem-solving, so I chose to look at the evidence and problem-solve, rather than spin in a state of worry and panic.

Milli Vanilli... with your song and dance about how all of my years of training and experience are still not enough for me to be an authority in my field... No, I do not need to keep proving myself... and no, the fraud police are not ready to arrest me. Unlike you, I am actually singing my own songs.

Persephone, you have been quite the challenge. One day you are working your magic and I am powerfully productive, and the next day you are holding me back with both hands. Let me just applaud you for your strength and let you know that I will only be listening to your adaptive aspects and not your maladaptive misalignments going forward.

Let's not forget VoD and all of the years she convinced me to not write a book. Bitch. Thankfully I turned her doubt upside down and got it done. Oh, and I'm doing it again by getting this workbook off the ground!

As we leave those days behind us, let's look forward to more time off for you in your new state of semi-retirement. You are allowed to voice your opinion under circumstances where my life may actually be in danger or in situations where sharing a signal might be truly beneficial, like reminding me to stay focused on my writing rather than scrolling social media.

The biggest difference is that now when you give me a signal, you will be pleasant and supportive rather than demeaning, degrading, and disrespectful. Oh, and no more fucking annoying ruminations and unnecessary noise. We are all done with that shit!

I recognize that all of this is new and that mistakes may be made as we navigate our way into this different way of doing things. We will be compassionate with ourselves and each other and will commit to communicating more effectively.

Thanks again for your service and I look forward to our continued evolution on this journey together.

Sincerely,
Chief Compassionate Asskicker

Here is a different letter, written by one of the participants in a Deep Dive Discussion Group:

Dear Fanny Faker and Zoe Energy Zapper,

I wanted to take some time to thank you for your service. You have faithfully shown up to keep me safe from danger, making mistakes or making a fool out of myself. You have served your positions well.

As the Head Honcho of this company, I am here to deliver a very special message. As of today, you are going home. Pack a bag and you are going on a much deserved vacation.

What you do now is all for you. I am taking over. No more nights of waking at 3am and looping until 4 or 5. No more doubting that I have the skills to navigate "scary" situations. I am breaking out and letting my light shine! In the words of Billy Joel, "I don't care what you say anymore, this is my life. Go ahead with your own life. Leave me alone."

Lovingly, Head Honcho

Now it's your turn to write your letter and here's the space to get it started:

Room for your own notes & reflections

Room for your own notes & reflections

Room for your own notes & reflections

Room for your own notes & reflections

Watch Your Language

Lean In

Lead

Bonus "L" Love Letters

Watch Your LANGUAGE

Let's get straight to the point. Here are some of my Language Pet Peeves:

Catastrophizing

Save "terrible" and "horrible" for tornados and hurricanes. It is not "the worst thing ever"... It sucks at this moment. That's all. Whatever emotionally challenging thing that happened did not "kill" you. You would not be reading this if it succeeded. You would be dead!

All or nothing

Stop using "always" and "never"... You may use "almost always" or "almost never" if you feel very strongly about this. "Perfect" or "disaster" are not your only options. Same with "success" or "failure"... Move away from the extremes!

For the love of whatever you love... stop **"shoulding"** on yourself!

You cannot, in fact, **"make sure"** of anything. "Being certain" and "in control" are illusions that your Inner Assholes use to manipulate you. Instead, you can do your best to increase the probability of a desirable outcome and then allow the situation to play out with confidence that you can deal with whatever happens.

Get rid of your big **"BUT..."** (which negates everything that comes before it).

Negative self-talk

If you wouldn't say it out loud to your best friend, don't say it to yourself! Your Action Step for this one is to notice when you are saying one of these out loud or to yourself... and STOP IT! If it helps to think about what I might do or say if I heard you (WWLS... What Would Lynn Say), then do that.

Work on language that is less extreme and less negative. Focus on language that is more realistic, mid-range, and compassionate.

You can write some of your catastrophizing and negative words here AND some alternatives that you will practice. Pages 37-41 in Aligned As F*ck provide you with some deeper dives into the subtleties of language.

Let's identify some words that you are willing to work on releasing from your vocabulary, and some new words to take their place.

I'll even get you started with some examples of my own...

My "No More" Words
(use these less often)

But
Should
Make sure
Perfect
Disaster
Can't

My "More Often" Words
(what to say instead)

And
Want to
Do my best
Good enough
Challenging situation
Don't want to

Now list your own:

NO MORE	MORE OFTEN

Lean in

Like it or not, life is not meant to be lived from the comfort of your couch or from the dopamine hits that you get from being the competent one in the room. Whatever way you have been using to delude yourself into pretending that comfort is king, it's time to change your thoughts as well as your habits.

Pick a "hard thing" that has been tripping you up — a situation where you feel discomfort. This could be a procrastination habit, an overdoing-for-others habit, or an "I should be (exercising, eating better, going to bed earlier)" habit.

Now notice what happens if you consider changing your habit. Do your Inner Assholes assert their opinion about this potential rocking of their ship? Of course they do! You are about to make their perceived job (keeping you safe) a whole lot harder.

They will continue to petition for you to listen to them, and they will keep trying to convince you to keep **False Comforting** by doing things the way they have always been done.

"False Comforts" are all of the things we think or do in an attempt to either appease or elude our Inner Assholes. This includes things like seeking reassurance ("Everything will be OK"), staying busy while worry nips at your heels, eating when you aren't actually hungry (comfort food), drinking to dull the senses, scrolling through social media, bingeing your streaming service of choice, and buying the next best thing that is going to solve all of your perceived problems.

You are welcome to keep following their orders and taking False Comfort every time you feel nervous, anxious, or uncomfortable. Let me know how that works out for you.

Another (hint: <u>better</u>) option is to take this Action Step and begin to lean into the discomfort.

Let's clarify that this is not an all-or-nothing situation. Part of why us anxious types struggle with this is because we buy into the cognitive distortion (all-or-nothing) that our Inner Assholes use for control.

You are not flipping a switch from off to on. You are learning to lean in by 1% at a time. Work up to changing the habit.

One more clarification: You are welcome to comfort yourself with any or all the things that are less than healthy for you, as long as you are doing them infrequently AND with intention. I'm not suggesting that you stop comforting yourself altogether. I am suggesting that you be aware of your habits of False Comfort and sprinkle them more intentionally rather than regularly.

Let's start by identifying one False Comfort habit that you may be willing to consider changing by leaning into it...

When I feel uncomfortable I have a habit of false comforting by:

Now let's look at one small step (think about taking 1% incremental steps) toward changing this False Comfort habit.

- If your habit is overdoing, overindulging, or over-the-top in some way, then think about one small step toward dialing it back.

- If your habit is under-doing, under-indulging, or under-performing in some way, then think about one small step toward some forward moving momentum.

I'll give you examples for each of these...

Over:
You have a loud Inner Critic who drives you to dictate to your family or employees all the things they "should" be doing at any given moment. It's like you are a cruise director. It feels great when you have all the answers... right up until the questions seem to never end and no one appears to be capable of doing any task without your input. This behavior is driven by the fear that if "everything" isn't done "right" then "something bad will happen."

One possible 1% step toward freedom and independence (for you and your family or employees) is to talk less. Be willing to be uncomfortable and let your family figure more things out on their own. What is the actual worst that could happen? As long as no one is dying, then dirty dishes and missed deadlines are actually great life learning lessons.

Under:

You say you want to lose weight. Maybe you have even purchased a program to guide and motivate you. Trouble is you can't get past your perfectionist to actually put the program to work.

First off I'm going to question your motivation. Focusing on being healthy will get you a lot further along than a goal to lose weight. Losing weight sounds like someone is "shoulding" and that's a tough habit to break.

Here is what you do to get some forward motion. You give yourself permission to do one small step each day. Pick one part of the program or one small aspect of your goal to have success with every day. Maybe it's increasing your intake of vegetables before you ever consider taking anything off your plate. Maybe it's walking for 1 minute longer than the day before (which does imply that you must walk for 1 minute the first day).

When you attempt to make too many changes all at once, it feels like failure, and you will quit because it feels uncomfortable. Don't quit! Simply lean in and take smaller steps!

Now it's your turn. **What is one small step you are willing to commit to that will support you in changing your false comforting habit?**

Lead

You have anthropomorphized your Inner Assholes. Now it's time to channel your Inner CEO to keep them in line!

Call it "Intuition," "Wise Mind," "Core Self," or "BadAss Bitch Boss." The name is less important (you can call it "Larry" or "Leah" if that works for you) than being connected to the part of you that knows what to do and when to do it.

This is not an easy step. We have been indoctrinated and conditioned to give our power over to others. Our Inner Assholes have perpetuated this power differential as protectors in our own damn mind.

That changes now!

Break your habit of holding back and deferring to the perceived power of someone or something "out there" and spend some time connecting with the part of you that is neutral and knowing.

Before we go any further, do you know the difference between your **Inner CEO** and your **Inner Office Manager**?

One of them gets curious, takes calculated risks, and knows that mistakes (and failures) are opportunities in disguise.

The other has a stick up its ass, tries to control everything and everyone, and pushes you to overdo it to the point of exhaustion.

Notice the difference?
Which one do you want to have in charge?

This can be a challenging endeavor, especially if you have never had a great boss. If you are concerned, know that you do not have to be a raving lunatic bitch boss. The best bosses LEAP (Lead with Empathy, Awareness, and Perspective).

Take a moment for this to sink in... You have a part that knows the deal, what's what, and why you are here on this planet at this time and in this life of yours. Wouldn't you rather have that part in charge rather than your Inner Critic, Voice of Doubt, Impostor, Perfectionist, or Anxiety?

So find a way that works for you to tap into that part of you that doesn't flip your cork over the little things. The part that doesn't avoid your feelings (which just makes them bigger and "badder" feeling feelings). The part that doesn't "need" to overcontrol with all of that crazy "making sure" and "shoulding" shit.

Yeah, yeah, you want some examples to prime your pump, don't you? This is where you may want to tap into more personal development stuff like:

- Spirituality
- What you believe about life and death
- Pondering stuff like your purpose (without puking) and "what's the fucking point?"
- Mindfulness
- Dealing with whatever deep shit your Inner Assholes may be using to convince you to avoid thinking about or dealing with the deep shit of life

Don't get your trousers in a twist. You can do this. Getting to this place is like climbing a mountain while it is still dark out. Uncomfortable, challenging, and even fear-inducing. Keep in mind though that the journey is worth it for that amazing view of the sunrise once you get to the top.

Action Step

Part One: Start your search for your Inner CEO by visualizing what a great leader looks like. If you want to get fancy, write up a resume or CV for your Inner Leader that showcases all of the qualities that you want your Inner Leader to possess.

Here are some examples of qualities that make great leaders:

Focused	Authentic	Generous
Open-Minded	Inspirational	Empowered
Innovative	Passionate	Accountable
Insightful	Personable	Stoic
Confident	Persistent	Great communicator
Patient	Decisive	

List the qualities you want in your Inner Leader:

Part Two: What personal development deep dives* are you willing to pursue to bring your unconscious to the surface?

* Caveat: you may only dive deep into personal development if you promise to do it from a place of self-compassion and understanding... NOT from a place of "I need to fix my broken self." You are not broken! You are perfectly imperfect.

Bonus L »→ Love Letters

In Aligned As F*ck, I suggested that you write a love letter to yourself. Did you do that one? Yeah, I didn't think so.

Here is your second chance, with a twist.

The actual suggestion (it wasn't an official ALIGNED Action Step) was to first write a letter to yourself from your Inner Assholes. Get out all of the mean, controlling, hurtful, uncomfortable, and disrespectful language that your Inner Assholes "speak" to you daily. Seriously, write that shit down in a letter from them to you.

WWMIAS (What Would My Inner Assholes Say):

Now read it back and feel all the feelings. Get pissed off. Would you let someone else speak to you that way? I think not!

Don't stop there. The next step is to write a rebuttal. Point by nasty point, get your Inner Allies to defend and support you. The truth will set you free. Show yourself love and compassion, just like you would a loved one.

My Rebuttal:

Finding yourself resisting this Bonus Action Step? Your Inner Assholes are not likely to let you do this one easily. Stand up to them and do it anyway!

Room for your own notes & reflections

Room for your own notes & reflections

Room for your own notes & reflections

Room for your own notes & reflections

Illuminate

Inspire

Ignite

Illuminate

The two definitions of Illuminate are:

- **Make something visible by shining a light on it**
- **Help to clarify or explain**

Let's do both of those...

This is one of the larger chapters in Aligned As F*ck. If you haven't read the book, I'll do a brief summary for you (while also highly recommending that you go read pages 49-59 there).

Your Inner Assholes represent the darker parts of your subconscious. Fear is the Grand Poobah and all of those feelings we label as negative are derivatives of it. It is an important part of our survival system AND, as I shared previously, these protectors sometimes take their job too seriously.

While we like to see ourselves as rational, logical beings, more often our behavior is actually driven by our emotions and our subconscious beliefs (shit we are not consciously aware of... yet).

Where do our beliefs come from? Our families, friends, teachers, society... basically from anyone and everyone who has ever influenced us!

At this point it is important to point out that dealing with your Inner Assholes requires you to stir up some shit from your past and your subconscious. If (and more likely when) this happens, please don't attempt to continue on this journey without support. Whether you seek a counselor, coach, your BFF, or me (in some ways I can be all three), deal with the shit rather than letting it stink up your life.

Let's get back to this Action Step. We're going to refer back to your Anthropomorphized character from the "A" chapter (so just fucking do that step if you skipped it). Remember to go through this process with one Inner Asshole at a time!

Now is the time to get to know those IAs even better. Tell their backstory. This is the Action Step from the "I" chapter in the book. If you did it when you read Aligned As F*ck, you are awesome and amazing and now you can add even more details to the backstories.

If you didn't get around to this step (or if you didn't read the book yet), you are still awesome and amazing, and here is your second chance to write out the backstories for any of the Inner Assholes that you have named.

Working out the backstories of your Inner Assholes helps you to bring out more of what is subconsciously sabotaging you, keeping you stuck (overdoing or undergoing), and overall making you feel sucky.

This is where we begin to change your narrative. You know, that story you tell yourself about yourself and all the shit that happens to you.

Yeah, we are going to change your perception of all of that, and your next step in that process is to sort out your Inner Assholes' backstories.

Let's talk just a little bit more about how this might look in your life.

I'll give you an example:

My Anxiety is Muci (the green snot blob bully character from the Mucinex ads). In the commercials he pushes his way into where he is not wanted, uses threatening language to get what he wants, and intimidates his host. "Obnoxious" and "bullying" are the top two words to describe him (and my Anxiety).

Muci reminds me of my maternal grandfather who was built like a linebacker. Not only did he not play football, he didn't get the opportunity to finish high school. My grandfather was a farmer who was embarrassed easily by the story he told himself about being a "dirt poor farmer," so he would put on a false bravado that included fancy suits and driving a Cadillac as a means to "prove" that he wasn't poor.

Even as a child, I could sense the fear and anxiety behind his facade. I used to hide his cigarettes (because they weren't healthy for him) and even though he would get mad, I somehow knew that he would just bluster and threaten, but nothing bad would actually happen. That's what it feels like when my Anxiety shows up attempting to bully me. I choose to "hide its cigarettes" by not giving in to its demands.

Let's say that you experience your Inner Asshole (like Anxiety) like a tornado that starts twirling. In order to avoid being sucked in, you put blinders on and buckle up, hoping that you can just get through your day to day without being torn to shreds.

Start by identifying that tornado as being like the Tasmanian Devil, but don't stop there. Think about how that character was pure impulse with no prefrontal cortex evolution. Now take it a step further and consider naming it something fun... like Tas or Tynnyfer,* and then consider how hard it is to not have a prefrontal cortex. How might you relate to it in a way that helps it learn, grow, and evolve?

You want another example, don't you?

Let's say that your Inner Critic shows up as a Cruise Director. Maybe you name her Candy. On one hand, Cruise Directors are fun, fashionable, and they have all of the facts. The trouble with being a Cruise Director is that all the others who are on the cruise (in your family, at work, etc.) expect you to have all of the answers all of the time. That's overwhelming. Candy will respond best to boundaries (which we will get to soon).

Now it's your turn to take this Action Step by filling in the backstories for your Inner Assholes.

Remember to do one at a time.
There is no pressure to overwhelm yourself!

---

* If you don't know who I mean by Tynnyfer, treat yourself to Season 6, Episode 4 "Doppelgängers" of Parks and Recreation.

My Inner Asshole's Backstory:
Come back to this step each time you discover another Inner Asshole.

Inspire

Without beating around the bush, this Action Step is to explore your **purpose** without puking. We are all here having this human experience. None of us is meant to have the exact same experience as anyone else.

Stop the comparisonitis, comparanoia, jealousy, and judgment (of self and others) that only leads you farther away from your own reason for living this one wild and precious life of yours.

Before we plow into purpose, and so as to decrease the probability of you puking, let's talk about **values.**

Figuring out your Top 3 values can be such a powerful tool in both finding your purpose and getting ALIGNED As F*ck! When you are clear on what is important to you, finding purpose, making decisions, and being aligned get a whole lot easier.

Part One: Look at a list of core values and circle your Top 3.

You can use this list of 50, or if none of these quite float your boat, do a Google Search for "Core Values List" and be prepared to be overwhelmed with options. Determining your core values is a big deal. When you know what is important to you, connecting to your purpose can be much clearer.

Core values list

Authenticity	Openness	Justice	Friendships
Competency	Self-Respect	Pleasure	Leadership
Happiness	Authority	Stability	Recognition
Loyalty	Curiosity	Beauty	Trustworthiness
Responsibility	Influence	Faith	Challenge
Achievement	Optimism	Kindness	Fun
Contribution	Service	Poise	Learning
Honesty	Autonomy	Status	Reputation
Meaningful	Determination	Boldness	Wealth
Work	Inner Harmony	Fame	Community
Security	Peace	Knowledge	Growth
Adventure	Spirituality	Popularity	Love
Creativity	Balance	Success	Respect
Humor	Fairness	Compassion	Wisdom

You may be tempted to choose more than 3. Keep in mind that many of these may resonate; however, we want to hone in on your Top 3 as a means to make your ALIGNED life easier.

Now, how do you connect with your purpose? Figure out what makes you cry!

Seriously, identify what makes you so connected to your emotions that you cry, then see how you can connect what you do (either for work or volunteer service) to the thing that lights you up.

Does the thing that makes you feel deep emotion have any connection to one or more of your Top 3 core values?

Want an example?

I cry when people are kind to each other, especially under challenging circumstances. One of my Top 3 core values is compassion.

Now you understand how I ended up counseling and coaching others through trying times!

Here's your Action Step:

I'm inspired by and find purpose in:

Ignite

We are almost ready to wrap up the last Action Step for this third section. I'm impressed that you are hanging in there. This work is not easy. Give yourself a pat on the back and know that I am rooting for you to keep up your momentum!

Making changes to our habits in thought and behavior is not an easy task. Too often we are caught in an all-or-nothing mindset and so we attempt to change everything all at once, and when our changes don't lead to relief immediately, we find ourselves and our Inner Assholes right back where we started, only even more frustrated and defeated.

Changing your thoughts and behaviors takes time. Start with 1% increments. Change one thing instead of twenty.

Recently I wanted to get into the habit of holding a plank position during my morning stretching routine. Instead of overwhelming myself with an unrealistic goal of even one minute, I started by holding a plank for 30 seconds. The next day I added 5 seconds. Then another 5 seconds each subsequent day. Once I got to 60 seconds, I allowed a few days of holding that amount. When I was ready, I started adding 5 seconds at a time again.

Do you see how instead of overwhelming myself and most likely quitting because of feeling fucking miserable and incompetent, I am now consistently holding a plank position for over one minute at a time?

I did the same thing years ago when I wanted to deal with my inability to journal.

While I know you are just chomping at the bit to get to the next Action Step, stay with me a moment. I promise it will be worth it. We are going to tackle your journaling jam, too.

Here is how it used to go for me. I would buy beautiful, inspiring, aesthetically pleasing journals, sometimes filled with motivating quotes. Then I would proceed to not write in them. Several years ago it clicked in my brain as to why I wasn't writing. We don't want to write "shitty" things in "pretty" journals.

Now we are getting to your Action Step:

Find yourself an ugly journal. I'm serious. I buy plain composition books (I buy several of them inexpensively at the back-to-school sales) and use a pencil or my least favorite colored pens from the pack.

Now that you have your **Dump Journal,** this is the one you will write all of the shit that your Inner Assholes taunt you with inside.

Each day (I do this first thing in the morning) go ahead and challenge yourself to write one page. What you write is way less important than getting into the habit of writing daily.

Some days I actually write down shit that I was spinning on in the middle of the night or when I woke up. Some days I write streams of consciousness. Some days I just write "Fuck" a lot.

Once I get the shit out by dumping it in my Dump Journal, I can be both creative and productive in the other places that I show up, like writing emails, social media posts, and books. I have more attractive notebooks where I can keep track of my ideas.

Commit to dumping your shit once a day. **Don't go back and look at it.** This is where you free up your head space by releasing the junk that your Inner Assholes use to distract you.

Why is this important?

Because processing the shit that comes up from our subconscious is a powerful way to go from feeling controlled by it to being in charge! Bring the subconscious to the surface so you can deal with it. (We will get to that soon!)

☐ *I will find an ugly notebook or a digital space like the Notes App on my phone, and commit to writing at least one sentence, paragraph, or page of shit once a day!*

SIGNATURE
_____

☐ *BONUS: I will also find a space to write out one thing that I am grateful for each day as a way to remember that life is made of both the challenging shit as well as the great shit!*

SIGNATURE
_____

Room for your own notes & reflections

Room for your own notes & reflections

Room for your own notes & reflections

Room for your own notes & reflections

Get Over It

Get On With It

Go Take Action

Get over it

If you haven't already gleaned this from the book and the ALIGNED Action Steps you have already done (you have done them, right?), part of why your Inner Assholes so easily manipulate you is that you take them too fucking seriously. Truth be told, you take yourself and all the "things" that happen "to" you way too seriously.

We are drama queens and kings, and our Inner Assholes use our desire to not only know "the rest of the story" but to be a star in the story as a means to control our attention and stifle our actions.

So when I say, "Get over it," you can read that as "Get over yourself!"

Nothing is happening "to" you. Things are happening. Tell your victim to shut the fuck up unless there is life or death in the queue. Use the opportunities in front of you to learn from mistakes, embrace what feels like a failure until you squeeze the diamond out of it, and just keep going (the start of the segue to the next Action Step).

All of that sounding a bit too harsh or aggressive? Bear with me…

In order to make changes in our thoughts and behaviors, we have to shake things up a bit.

Think of it like a pendulum that is stuck on one extreme. In order to get it going and swinging in an arc that is efficient and effective, you must first push it to the other extreme.

By going from believing all of the shit your Inner Assholes dish up to telling those drama queens/kings to shut the fuck up, you make a space to come to better terms with them.

No more sympathy or reassurance. Instead switch to empathy and compassion for them (which means for yourself). You have *acknowledged, accepted,* and *anthropomorphized* them. You know their backstory and motivations. Now is the time to peel back their distracting drama, and gain a new perspective on their shenanigans.

So give your victim a hug. Remind them that you appreciate them. Now firmly guide them from center stage to back stage so that you can move to the next action step in getting ALIGNED As F*ck!

I am ready to admit that I take the following thing way too seriously and I commit to changing my perception of this situation to one of more neutrality:

Get on with it

Stop mentally masturbating and make a decision. You will never have all of the information, or the perfect time, or whatever bullshit your Inner Assholes feed you to keep you spinning in circles chasing your own "should shit."

We will go into the Deep Dive of Decision Making later in the workbook AND I'm going to prime your pump on this one right here.

Move forward. Failure is not the end of everything. It's the beginning of another thing.

Your Action Step here is to **pick a place where you have been feeling stuck and make the decision to move forward and get the fuck out of being stuck.**

"Being stuck" can mean both *stuck in inaction* (overthinking and underdoing) or *stuck in overaction* (overdoing and under being). Either one is you avoiding taking intentional action that may actually get you closer to whatever you want.

Knowing what you want and taking the action to get it may not sound like such a big deal. For so many of us, though, it is a big, fat, hairy, scary deal! Our Inner Assholes do not allow for us to want anything for ourselves. That would be selfish, and someone along the way once accused us of being selfish, so we will have none of that, thank you very much!

Action Step:

Identify what you want, because next up is how to make a plan to take the action needed to actually get what you want.

This want can be internal or external. Big or small. Simple or complex.

Patience. A new car. Peace of mind. A puppy. Health. A new job. Freedom from anxiety. Ice cream. Fulfillment. Money.

The key here is to start with a "want" that you are willing to play with. Getting what you want doesn't have to be hard and it doesn't have to take a long time. It does take some effort on your part. See what you can do to pick one thing and then check out the next Action Step for some steps for bringing your want into your reality.

One thing* that I'm willing to admit that I want:
(keep it simple to start if that feels safer)

---

* This is another one of the Action Steps that you can come back to as many times as necessary

Go take action

You are currently stuck on figuring out what you want, aren't you? Take a step back and pick something simple that you want.

Even the most talented people had to practice to get to the top of their field. You will have to practice these Action Steps to get ALIGNED As F*ck, just like any other superstar.

Seriously, pick something simple to start with.

Once you have an idea of what that thing is, it's time to figure out the path to connect where you are (without what you want) to where you will be once you have what you want.

Action Step:

Start by visualizing what your life will be like when you have what you want.
Now, let's reverse engineer a plan of action.

Here's an example:

I wanted to write a workbook to be a companion to the book I wrote a year ago.

Now that wasn't enough, I had to tie it to a deeper, meaningful "Why." So I visualized it. My visualization included me seeing your smiling face as your life transforms through your new thoughts and actions.

How did I get from no workbook to your smiling face? One step at a time.

I considered what it would take for you to be smiling and feeling successful after completing all of the Action Steps. Then I considered which Action Steps would result in you feeling successful. Shit got real when I contemplated which Action Steps you might be willing to complete.

Then I worked on a shitty rough draft because my Inner Assholes wouldn't let me write another book (even a workbook), so I played the game of "I'm not writing a book, I'm simply writing a shitty first draft" game.

The only other step here was for me to commit to spending time each day actually writing the Action Steps that support you in transforming your Inner Assholes into Allies.

Oh yeah, and I needed to minimize overthinking and distracting myself... because let's be honest, I'm not as disciplined as I might seem. So I gave myself grace and compassion and I did my best to get from here (where there was no workbook AND I wanted there to be a workbook) to there (where you are smiling and feeling successful having completed the Action Steps from this workbook).

Taking intentional steps of action rather than the obligatory "burden of busy" that over-functioners tend to gravitate toward is a key component here.

Now it's your turn. **You already wrote down what you want.** (You did that step in the last section, correct?) **Now write down the steps you are willing to take to make it real.**

A couple of caveats:

- Do the work to figure out what you want... Don't use any obligatory things that you think you are supposed to want or "should" want.

- Start simple.

- Practice, practice, practice.

If this shit was easy, everyone would be doing it and I would be out of a job, so practice grace and compassion with yourself!

Steps I will take to move toward what I want:

Bonus G »→ Growth Mindset

Back in the late 1980s when I was an undergraduate in psychology and early childhood education, I did a research project measuring the roles of intelligence and effort in the classroom. I don't remember the specifics, but I do know that unbeknownst to me, others were also curious about this mindset phenomenon. Stanford psychologist Carol Dweck published some of the first real research in the area she termed **Growth Mindset** in the 1990s.

The simplified explanation of fixed vs. growth mindset relates to what you believe about your intelligence, talent, and other internal qualities.

- Those with a "fixed" mindset believe that intelligence and talent are innate and that they cannot be changed.

- Those with a "growth" mindset recognize that intelligence, talent, and other qualities can be developed with practice and effort.

There has been much insight into what we thought we knew about how to motivate and encourage our children (and ourselves), and how we too often miss the mark by focusing on the adjective labels like "smart," "intelligent," "talented," "musical," "athletic," and "scholarly." Unfortunately research has shown feedback that focuses on labels actually backfires.

When feedback about performance is presented using <u>verbs</u> rather than <u>adjectives</u> (labels), people actually perform better in their future endeavors.

What does this look like? Focusing on qualities like effort, persistence, problem solving, and rising to a challenge instead of outcome help us to perform better.

You are getting this taste of the concept of growth mindset here as it came to my attention that I had not talked about this specifically yet in the workbook, and it is one of my favorite and useful mindset tools by far.

You will notice that it is infused in most of this Inner-Asshole-to-Allies work. Now you have a name for it!

Growth mindset is freedom

Perseveres in the face of failure
Knows effort is required to build new skills
Finds inspiration in others' success
Embraces challenges
Accepts criticism
Has a desire to learn
Builds abilities

Fixed mindset is limiting

Avoids challenges
Gives up easily
Feels threatened by others' success
Desires to look smart
Feels effort is fruitless
Ignores feedback
Has fixed abilities

It is possible to have a fixed mindset in one area of our life and a growth mindset in another. Our Inner Assholes would like to keep us stuck in fixed mindset FUBAR (Fucked Up Beyond All Repair). Part of the work you are doing to transform those IAs into Allies is to embrace a growth mindset in more areas of your life.

To that means, your Action Step here is to notice where your mindset is more fixed and where it may already be more growth oriented.

Action Step:

Do your own research into Growth Mindset.
Bonus Points: Research "Stress Enhancing Mindset" as well.

Room for your own notes & reflections

Room for your own notes & reflections

Room for your own notes & reflections

Room for your own notes & reflections

No Means No, Not Maybe

No Judgment

No Excuses

No means no, not maybe

As you continue to do this **personal development work** (there, I said it, getting ALIGNED As F*ck is personal development work), it will be important for you to practice saying "No" or "Not right now" to the demanding people in your outer world (children, spouse, boss, colleagues, friends, clients, random strangers on the street) AND to those IA naysayers who nag at you in your own head.

The boundaries you set within yourself are the most important and powerful boundaries you can form. Resisting the tempting urges put forth by your Inner Assholes can be tricky and oh-so worth it in the end.

Right now I am choosing to resist the urge to distract myself with any number of tempting activities. Instead of writing I could be scrolling through social media, taking my empty tea mug to the sink where I would find dishes that "need" to be washed, making a meal, doing laundry, working on an email to my list, checking on the volunteer work that I do for my daughter's school, cuddling with the dogs, letting the goats out to play, or checking my email.

My Inner Assholes can find justification for any of those important activities (and more).

My Inner CEO, however, knows that while all of those activities have value, they are not currently urgent and that the impulse to distract myself lies deeper.

For my business to evolve and flourish, I have to accomplish certain important tasks. The most recent one was to finish the rough draft of this workbook so that I could begin the testing phase which would then lead to publishing the workbook so that I can get it into your hands.

Finishing the workbook (or any major project) meant that it would be time for me to step up and be seen again.

Ugh!

Finishing the draft was more important than the dishes getting washed. The dogs and goats could get the attention they deserve during scheduled breaks, and my life was actually much more peaceful and efficient when I only checked email and social media at set times throughout the day.

Those other activities, though, can be used to stay small and remain unseen.

Whether driven by your Inner Perfectionist or one of your other dramatic divas, be aware of the tug to keep you off-task. Keeping you off the stage and out of sight by keeping you busy is quite the scare tactic.

Is the goal here to go from no boundaries to being a 100% locked down and boundary-focused wunderkind?

Nope, so shake off that all-or-nothing shit and choose to take this Action Step with 1% incremental steps at a time.

This is a great time to revisit those core values that you identified on page 37.

When you struggle to set either an internal or external boundary, ask yourself if the activity in front of you supports your values. If your answer is "No," then your response is "No" or "Not right now."

Name one situation where you will say "No" or "Not Right Now" to either your Inner Assholes or to someone who needs to hear that from you at work or at home.

No judgment

How often have you finally gotten the "quiet time" that you were dreaming about – free of the demands from family, friends, or work – only to find that you did none of the "things" that you thought you wanted to do while you were busy doing something else for someone else, only to end up doing nothing satisfying for yourself?

You are driven by feeling accomplished, by feeling that the work you do has purpose, and by thinking of yourself as someone competent.

You are making your Inner Assholes' jobs easy by confusing **purpose-driven** and **obligation-driven.**

Getting caught up in what you "should" do, rather than what you want to do, is one of the most common challenges on the struggle bus.

The Action Step for No Judgment is simple:

Stop Shoulding on Yourself!

That's it. Notice when you are thinking about what you "should" do. Then ask yourself if you really want to do it.

Now I know what your Inner Assholes are doing right now. They are doing their damnedest to shift the "should" to "need" instead of "want." We can't just all go around only doing what we want to do, because there are all manner of things that need to be done. Right?

You are welcome to keep playing the excuses game and giving in to your Inner Assholes' "should." I'm not here to twist your arm. I am here to help you see a different path. A different way of seeing how this game can be played... and won!

When you consciously choose to do the things that "need" to be done (like laundry, a work project, or your taxes), not because you "should" but because you "want" to do them, your stress level will decrease.

"Should" comes with struggle.

"Need" makes you feel nagged.

"Want" gives you wisdom and power!

I want to do the laundry (or delegate it to be done) because it reminds me that I have clothing I love and want to take care of it. I am grateful for the opportunity to be responsible for the clothes that I purchased with the money that I spent time and energy acquiring.

I want to finish this workbook (my work project) because I know there are people like yourself who will benefit from the wisdom and words I am sharing.

Believe it or not, I even want to do my taxes because that is the symbol of living in a country where I have freedom of choice (relative to less democratic countries) and where I contribute my part to public services that we too often take for granted.

So notice how often you are **shoulding** on yourself and others and simply STOP IT!

Not that easy? Still have a part that wants to take a stand and resist this one?

Reframe:

"It shouldn't be raining" ➤➤ *"Rain cleans the city and helps plants grow."*

"I should take care of my aging parents" ➤➤ *"I am willing to take care of my aging parents AND take care of myself while doing so."*

"I should be getting more work done" ➤➤ *"I am a human being, not a human doing."*

How about meeting your IAs halfway with a middle step, or ask that resistant and resentful part what would make them more willing to take the step.

Name one thing you are willing to stop complaining about and move toward "want" or "willing to" instead:

No Excuses

How happy are your Inner Assholes right now? I'm suspecting that you have crossed the line and that they are doing their best to throw excuses and justifications like monkeys throwing shit at the zoo!

If you haven't already noticed, let me share this important point. **To get what you want, you have to start by identifying and clarifying what it is that you actually want.**

You are welcome to keep reading through this workbook without doing the Action Steps. You aren't going to get very far without doing the work, though. Just saying...

When you are ready to stop pretending that your "reasons" and "valid justifications" are anything more than bullshit excuses, then you will be ready for this Action Step!

Acknowledge your reasons and valid justifications for what they really are and then flip your script.

"Flipping your script" is a way to go from focusing on the negative (all of the reasons that what you want won't work) to focusing more on the positive (reasons to move forward anyway).

Here is a fear-based fear of failure excuse:

"I can't hire anyone to help expand my business because I might not be able to afford it."

Here is an empowering flipped script:

"Hiring someone to help my business expand will provide the growth needed to financially support the hiring and expansion."

Want more examples? I got you covered:

"Social media marketing sucks so I'm not doing it!" ➻ *"My ideal clients are on (fill in the social media platform of choice), so I will take a course and put what I learn into action so that my ideal clients can find me."*

"I have to do all the family laundry because my kid (or significant other) won't do it right." ➻ *"Learning to do laundry is an important life skill and if their clothes aren't cleaned well, they will either learn to do it better or live with it."*

"I don't have the time to be creative. I have work to do." ➻ *"Creativity comes in many forms and I choose to spend at least an hour a day engaging in my version of creative."*

Your turn...

Write down your Top 2 Excuses, then flip your script:

MY BULLSHIT EXCUSES	MY FLIPPED SCRIPT

Room for your own notes & reflections

Room for your own notes & reflections

Room for your own notes & reflections

Embrace the Process

Embarrassment Won't Kill You

Enter Humor Stage Left

Embrace the process

How do you feel about failure? No one really likes to fail; however, some folks have figured out that failure is part of the process on the road to success. They are the ones who enjoy their success with less stress!

Your Inner Assholes may scream at you like one of the characters in Apollo 13. The funny thing is, that line, "Failure is not an option," was made up for the movie. No one actually said that in real life.

Failure is *always* an option. **Pretending to ignore, resist, or avoid it will keep you stuck in perfectionistic purgatory.**

Being open to failure will take you much farther along your path.

But how do you get used to failure as an option for learning and growth?
You plan to fail.

Yep, your Action Step here is to plan for failure.

Changing your mindset around "failure" requires you to stop thinking about it and start doing something to prove to your Inner Assholes that the fear of failure will no longer hold you hostage.

When I wrote the book ALIGNED As F*ck, I got past my Inner Assholes by planning for that manuscript to just be a shitty first draft that would never make it to a publisher. I consciously chose to stay in the moment and simply write without the pressure of whether what I was writing would end up winning or losing.

Had I stayed stuck in thoughts about whether I would fail or succeed, I might still be spinning, and you would not have benefitted from that book, or this workbook!

Since I know that this is a really tough one for most people, I'll give you another example before I ask you to take the Action Step.

If taking a big leap and potentially landing with a belly flop is too much for you to start, look for something smaller to begin this practice.

BTW, just because you practice planning-to-fail does not mean that you will fail. This exercise is really about being willing to fail, not forcing a failure.

Here are a few other pointers as you take this step:

- *Allow yourself the discomfort of thinking through a situation where you are afraid of failing, then make a plan for your next step if that failure occurs.*

- *Recognize where you get stuck in indecision (we will deal with that soon) and how that feeds your fear.*

- *Make a commitment to yourself to keep going even when you feel like you are falling and failing.*

Here are those examples I promised:

- *Your fear keeps you from investing time and energy into expanding to a next-level project for your business out of fear that you are the only one who thinks it's a good idea, or fear that no one will buy your product or service.*

- *You hold yourself back from any opportunity that could be perceived as competitive for fear of being publicly humiliated when you "lose." (The extra bonus here is your own story that you "wasted your time" if you didn't actually "win.")*

- *You say you want to be in good physical shape, yet fear of failure keeps you stuck in old eating and exercise habits.*

- *You want to be connected to others, but a fear about not inviting people to your house keeps your front door closed.*

- *You've had a major change (like divorce) in your life and are letting fear of another "failure" keep you from doing fun stuff, like traveling with your kids or dating.*

Now it's time to choose your own scenario where your Inner Assholes are using your fear of failure to hold you hostage, and then make a plan for what you will do if you "fail."

If I had "failed" with my book, my plan was to keep going and keep writing until I had a draft that contained the wisdom, wit, and words that satisfied me. When you know in your soul that you have something to offer or something important to do, you don't stop when things get hard. If you only want what you want if it comes easily, I suggest you dig deeper into why you think you want an outcome only if it doesn't require discomfort.

Action Step:

What am I holding myself back from because of my fear of failure?

Is the fear of embarrassment teaming up with your fear of failure to keep you stuck? Take this Action Step first and we will deal with embarrassment next!

Embarrassment won't kill you

This one is pretty straightforward. No matter what society and your Inner Assholes tell you, feeling embarrassed will not kill you. Do you really wish that you were dead because you are uncomfortable? No, you just wish that you could make the uncomfortable feeling go away at that moment.

I could keep going with this explanation about being willing to feel embarrassed AND we both know where this is leading, so let's just go straight there...

Your Action Step for this one is to purposefully put yourself in an embarrassing situation.

Not ready to tackle this action step quite so quickly?

Look, every single person on this planet has done at least one embarrassing thing in their life. (And likely a whole heap more.) No one is meant to be perfect, and embarrassing situations are actually great opportunities for growth.

Reframe "embarrassed" to "empowered" by considering that making others laugh reduces their stress. (You know, "laughter is good medicine.") Why not join in the laughter yourself and even get your Inner Allies to join the fun!

I'm going to give you a little space to breathe. For now, just write down the embarrassing scenario, because in the next section you will get a tool that will help you accomplish this Action Step a little more easily.

My embarrassing scenario:

Enter humor stage left

Whether or not you were born with a resting bitch face, it's time to dig deep and find your funny bone.

One of my all-time favorite movies is Life is Beautiful. The main character uses humor and imagination to help his son survive the horrors of WWII in a concentration camp. If he could do it under those conditions of actual life and death, then you can figure out how to do it no matter what challenges you are facing.

Am I suggesting that your challenges aren't challenging enough? Nope. I am suggesting that perspective is important and that using humor to get your Inner Assholes to dial down the intensity of any situation is a key component in getting ALIGNED As F*ck! So take a look at the situation you chose in the last section and how embarrassment would like to overlay the situation. Now tell me... how are you going to bring humor into the mix?

You want an example, don't you?

There was a time when I worried about standing up in front of a group of people. I even had a presentation go more like a train wreck, so my Inner Assholes had "evidence" that I would embarrass myself if I tried public speaking again.

What helped me get back in front of a crowd? Joking about how they might see pit stains on my shirt as I had forgotten to put on deodorant that morning.

By humorously sharing with the group that I was nervous, I took the wind out of my Inner Assholes' sails.

Now what can you do to bring humor to a potentially embarrassing situation and empower yourself?

How I will bring humor to the situation:

Room for your own notes & reflections

Room for your own notes & reflections

Room for your own notes & reflections

Room for your own notes & reflections

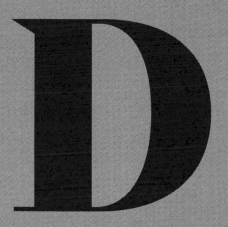

Discern

Decide

Deal with It or Delegate It or Dump It

Discernment

Your thoughts and feelings are just that – thoughts and feelings. When you give them too much credit or assume they are "right," you get caught up in a whole heap of ridiculous reacting.

Reacting is great when you are actually in a dangerous situation. It's hard-wired into your survival system. However, most of the time you are just uncomfortable and a response would be a much better choice at the moment.

While sometimes only a few seconds differentiate a **response** from a **reaction**, those few seconds can make all the difference in the outcome!

When you discern your Inner Assholes' signals (when they are actually protecting you or helping you) from their obnoxious noise (when they are protecting you from situations that are not dangerous, only uncomfortable) you will have turned a corner in your relationship with your Inner Allies.

This Action Step will need some energy directed specifically toward your Inner Critic, as discernment works best when judgment is left out of the process!

You are here because shit like values, vision, purpose, and passion – all the stuff of Personal Development – floats your boat. This is the deep stuff AND you are up for the challenge!

What is your Action Step here?

"Practice, practice, practice…" the mantra of personal development. Practice shifting to neutral in situations where your Inner Assholes are shouting, so that you can easily discern whether they are actually sending you an important signal, or whether they are simply being noisy little fuckers.

> ☐ *I will practice noticing whether my Inner Assholes are truly being Allies and warning me about something important or whether they are being overprotective and obnoxious with their noise.*
>
> SIGNATURE
> _____

Decide

You can choose not to decide, but that, in and of itself, is a choice. Floating on the boat of indecision makes me nauseous and even more anxious.

Just because you make a decision does not mean that you cannot change your mind. (Your Inner Assholes don't want you to know that part of the process.) Keeping all the options open all the time simply leads to overwhelm. Learn to make the best decision that you can at any moment, AND stay open to making a different decision from a neutral place if your first decision is not working out for you.

Decisions are best made from that place of neutrality and with the guidance of your Inner CEO. You've done the work through the Actions Steps in this workbook that will help you connect with your Inner CEO and make decisions like a champ.

Get over the idea that you can make the "right" decision every damn time. Choose to stay in the moment and make decisions based on those values that you identified earlier in this process.

Feelings are not facts. Allowing yourself to get caught up in the feelings or thinking twenty steps ahead will actually lead to less successful decisions.

Shift into neutral, which is where you can more logically access your thoughts, feelings, and values. From that place, make a choice.

You cannot be certain. You can give yourself the space to decide, and then make another decision if the first one does not work out. **Remember that failure and mistakes are just opportunities in disguise.**

This step may be especially useful if you are of an age (typically over 40) where embarrassment is no longer a driving force used by your Inner Assholes, because you easily say, "Fuck it." However, those evolving little fuckers get you with second-guessing.

Decisions are made harder when fear says, "If you make the wrong choice you will be fucked forever!"

Maybe you spent inordinate amounts of time being influenced and affected by the dumbass decisions of others and your Inner Assholes act as if you could possibly make a dumbass decision.

Let's see... nope, not possible.

You are not a dumbass! Think about the person who caused you pain and discomfort. Can you actually see yourself making a decision along those same lines? Maybe at one time in your life, but not likely now.

Those people are making decisions impulsively and from a maladaptive place. You are not them.

You are making decisions that align with your values and from an adaptive place as you transform your Inner Assholes into Allies!

Is it possible for you to make a dumbass decision? Yeah, because anything is possible. The more important question is whether it is probable. The answer to that, my friend, is a resounding "No!"

Keep in mind that there are decisions that can bump you off track for a blip in time, and ones that can fuck up your life forever. Trust your Inner CEO to discern the difference.

So you may make a decision that will not work out for you AND you still have the tools and insights (or at the very least you are beginning to connect with them) to keep making decisions until the outcome works out in your favor.

If you have trouble getting your brain into neutral, do this hack: **Go play a moderately challenging game and then go back to the decision and make your choice.**

Need another decision-making hack? **Pretend that the decision is not about you, but about your friend instead.** When we step outside of our own emotions (and the influence of our Inner Assholes) – like when helping a friend make a decision – we make decisions more objectively and from a variety of perspectives. So pretend the decision is for a friend instead of for you.

Demanding another hack, are you?

Grab a snack and head to a dark space. Making decisions on an empty stomach doesn't work so well, so having a snack and getting rid of distractions in a dark room may help you make that decision you have been struggling with making.

Now that you have a few possible hacks, your Action Step is:

Practice making decisions. You can start with little ones like: Vanilla, Chocolate, Twist, or "No thanks, I'm lactose intolerant."

Write down at least one decision you have been wrestling with... and then make that decision! Check each one off when you have finished making your decision:

Deal with it, or delegate it, or dump it

Here we are at the last Action Step, so we are going to wrap this all up like a burrito. Time to stop seeking certainty and comfort. Find your Inner CEO, and change your relationship with those Inner Assholes.

That means you have to **Deal with It.** Trust that no matter what comes across your path, you can figure it out and handle it.

Dealing with something does <u>not</u> mean you have to like it.

Let's be clear that I am not saying that you must deal with EVERYTHING ALL OF THE TIME. There are definitely things that you can delegate or even dump from your mile-long To Do List.

Your Inner Assholes will tell you otherwise. Your Anxiety will tell you that you "need" to do all the things to feel safe. Your Inner Critic will then tell you that you are doing it "wrong." Your Impostor will chime in with all the ways you need to "prove" yourself to avoid being found out as a fraud. Your Voice of Doubt (VoD) will show up no matter what you do (or don't do).

You've done the work and have a better understanding that your Inner Assholes are misguided in their attempts to control you and keep you safe.

Now it's time to bring all of the work that you have done together as you teach your Inner Allies some better social skills!

Pick one of those Decisions that you made in the last Action Step and make your Plan for the Worst. Write out all of the ways your Inner Assholes will attempt to sabotage you (since you know them so well at this point).

What will you do if any (or all) of their "What ifs...?" come true? Write out how you will deal with each and every one of them.

My Plan for the Worst:

Now paint a picture of the best possible outcome.

My Expectation for the Best:

From here forward as you make progress toward *what you want*, what aligns with *your core values*, and what you have decided is *yours to pursue*, you have your **Plan** if anything "bad" happens.

Don't think about the plan (which would be worrying). Simply remind your Inner Assholes (when they attempt to play "What if...?" with you, and they will) that there is a plan in place AND that their job is to support you in reaching your expectations of the **Best Possible Outcome.**

Plan for the worst & expect the best!

Holy Shit! You made it to the end of this ALIGNED As F*ck Action Step Workbook!

Give yourself a hearty pat on the back and a celebratory "Woop Woop!"
(Just suggestions... you are welcome to celebrate in whatever way works best for you!)

It has been a pleasure working through this Alignment process with you. I trust you found most if not all of it useful in transforming your Inner Assholes into more helpful Allies.

I know that this work can be challenging to do on your own, especially since your Inner Assholes may not be cooperating in the process.

That's why I offer workshops, groups, training, and individual sessions to support you in transforming your Inner Assholes into Allies.

Questions, concerns, or seeking more support?

Reach out to me at: lynn@lynndutrow.com

Acknowledgments

Heartfelt gratitude from me to the following folks who invested in a Deep Dive Discussion Group or in some other manner provided me with valuable feedback as part of the editing process for this companion workbook:

Ana	Jodi	Melissa
Deborah	Kelli	Mikah
Demi	Kristine	Rachel
Donna	Laura	Rebecca C.
Helene	Leah	Rebecca F.
Ikenna	Lisa	Safrianna
Jana	MacKenzie	Sherry

Staff at Curious Iguana, Dancing Bear, Turn the Page, and Pump & Rye

Thank you for being so fucking awesome!

Room for your own notes & reflections

Room for your own notes & reflections

Room for your own notes & reflections

Room for your own notes & reflections

Room for your own notes & reflections

Room for your own notes & reflections

Room for your own notes & reflections

Room for your own notes & reflections

Room for your own notes & reflections

Room for your own notes & reflections

Room for your own notes & reflections

Room for your own notes & reflections

Room for your own notes & reflections

Made in the USA
Middletown, DE
28 October 2023

41448285R00064